To our precious children—
Rob, Claire, Brittnye, and Ashley

Photo Credits include: Cleo Photography–pages 7,19 and 21; From *A Week in the Life of the LCMS*–pages 11 and 33; Roy Gumpel/TSI–page 35.

Scripture quotations are taken from the HOLY BIBLE, NEW INTERNATIONAL VERSION®. NIV®. Copyright © 1973, 1978, 1984 by International Bible Society. Used by permission of Zondervan Publishing House. All rights reserved.

Copyright © 1999 Concordia Publishing House

3558 S. Jefferson Avenue, St. Louis, MO 63118-3968

Manufactured in China

1 2 3 4 5 6 7 8 9 10   08 07 06 05 04 03 02 01 00 99

THE
ABC's
of
CHRISTIAN
PARENTING

Twenty-six ways to love and nurture
your child today and every day

Robert & Debra Bruce

CPH.
Concordia Publishing House

*A*ffirm

your child every day as a gift

from God, no matter what

yesterday's problems were.

If you, then, though you are evil, know
how to give good gifts to your children,
how much more will your Father in heaven
give good gifts to those who ask Him!

Matthew 7:11

Build

upon your child's talents,

seeking to discover

God's plan for him.

To one he gave five talents of money,
to another two talents, and to another
one talent, each according to his ability.

Matthew 25:15

Communicate

with your child

in a way that glorifies Christ,

always asking before speaking,

"Would I say this to a friend?"

Glory to God in the highest.

Luke 2:14

**D**edicate

yourself to the body of Christ

through commitment to a

congregation, regular worship

attendance, Bible study,

prayer, and service.

Then David said to the whole assembly,
"Praise the LORD your God." So they all
praised the LORD, the God of their fathers;
they bowed low and fell prostrate before
the LORD and the king.

1 Chronicles 29:20

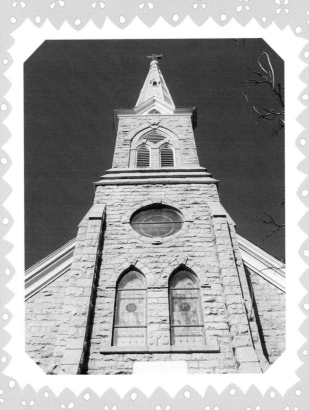

*E*xercise

self-control when you're angry,

committing your feelings to the Lord

rather than using them

against your child.

"In your anger do not sin": Do not let the sun
go down while you are still angry.

Ephesians 4:26

Forgive

your child's wrongdoings

as the Lord forgives you,

and start over together with

God's grace and love.

Forgive us our debts, as we also
have forgiven our debtors.

Matthew 6:12

Give

your child everything she needs

instead of everything she wants, even

if you have to say no sometimes.

Your Father knows what you need
before you ask Him.

Matthew 6:8

Hug

your child 10 times every day,

especially when he is unlovable.

A warm touch can erase even

the largest strain in a relationship.

And He took the children in His arms,
put His hands on them and blessed them.

Mark 10:16

Include

Bible study and prayer time

in your daily family routine,

and challenge your child

to do the same.

For where two or three come together
in My name, there am I with them.

Matthew 18:20

Join

in agreement with your spouse,

and stand firm together on rules,

expectations, and discipline.

Children, obey your parents in the Lord,
for this is right.

Ephesians 6:1

Keep

commitments you make outside

your home, so your child can

observe as you model responsibility.

Above all, my brothers, do not swear—
not by heaven or by earth or by anything
else. Let your "Yes" be yes, and your
"No," no, or you will be condemned.

James 5:12

Live

each day to the fullest,

appreciating the beauty of God's

world and the hope of your faith,

instead of hurrying through the day.

Whatever is lovely, ...
think about such things.

Philippians 4:8

Manage

aspects of your child's life

that could lead to stress, such

as too much activity or television

or inappropriate freedoms.

When I was a child, I talked like a child,
I thought like a child, I reasoned like a child.
When I became a man, I put childish
things behind me.

1 Corinthians 13:11

Nurture

your child lovingly

so he can experience God

through your example.

How good and pleasant it is when
brothers live together in unity!

Psalm 133:1

Open

up doors of opportunity

for your child as you encourage

the development of his skills

through education.

Do not neglect your gift,
which was given you.

1 Timothy 4:14

$\mathscr{P}$atiently

wait upon the Lord

as He answers prayers

for you and your child.

Blessed are all who wait for Him!

Isaiah 30:18

Question

the reasons for your child's

unacceptable behavior as you look

beyond the act to its root causes.

Wisdom is supreme; therefore get wisdom.
Though it cost all you have,
get understanding.

Proverbs 4:7

Respect

your child as an individual

rather than as an extension of you

or your spouse.

A little child will lead them.

Isaiah 11:6

Strive

to create quality time

with your child every day that

enables you to listen to her joys,

hopes, concerns, and fears.

Teach us to number our days aright,
that we may gain a heart of wisdom.

Psalm 90:12

Trust

God to guide you

as you prayerfully make

daily parenting decisions.

If you believe, you will receive
whatever you ask for in prayer.

Matthew 21:22

Ultimately,

trust your child when he leaves

home, knowing you have fulfilled

your commitment to God

as a Christian parent.

Blessed is the man who perseveres under
trial, because when he has stood the test,
he will receive the crown of life.

James 1:12

Verbalize

your thoughts and feelings

when you're happy or sad,

letting your child know

you are still approachable.

In everything set them an example
by doing what is good. In your teaching
show integrity, seriousness and soundness
of speech that cannot be condemned.

Titus 2:7–8

Wait

patiently for your child

to pass through stages,

realizing that some behaviors,

while unpleasant, are quite normal.

Let us run with perseverance the race
marked out for us.

Hebrews 12:1

E𝑋pect

the best from your child at home,

at school, and at play, while also

extending grace for human frailty.

For we know in part and we prophesy
in part, but when perfection comes,
the imperfect disappears.

l Corinthians 13:9–10

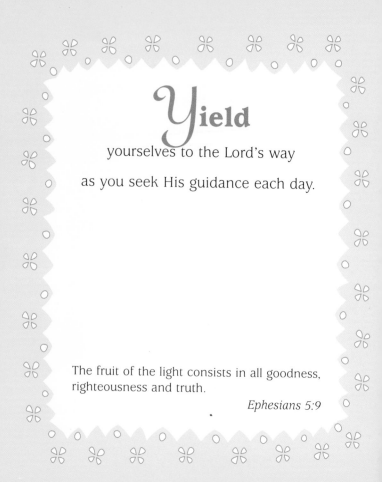

Yield

yourselves to the Lord's way

as you seek His guidance each day.

The fruit of the light consists in all goodness, righteousness and truth.

Ephesians 5:9

Zealously

start each day in prayer and praise,

marveling at God's work

in the life of your family.

Whatever you do, work at it with all your
heart, as working for the Lord, not for men.
Colossians 3:23